marty mcguire

marty mcguire

BY *Kate Messner*

ILLUSTRATED BY *Brian Floca*

SCHOLASTIC INC.

NEW YORK TORONTO LONDON AUCKLAND

SYDNEY MEXICO CITY NEW DELHI HONG KONG

This book is being published simultaneously in hardcover by Scholastic Press.

Library of Congress Cataloging-in-Publication Data

Messner, Kate.

Marty McGuire / by Kate Messner ; illustrated by Brian Floca. — 1st ed. p. cm.

Summary: When tomboy Marty is cast as the princess in the third-grade play, she learns about improvisation, which helps her become more adaptable.

[1. Theater—Fiction. 2. Schools—Fiction.] I. Floca, Brian, ill.

II. Title. PZ7.M5615Mar 2011 [Fic]—dc22 2010031291

ISBN 978-93-5471-661-4

First paperback printing, May 2011

This reprint edition, July, 2023

Printed in India at Shivam Offset Press, New Delhi

For Tom, with love and laughter

—K.M.

For Samantha, Jay, Ella,

and Mira

—B.F.

chapter 1

That nice Mrs. Kramer lied to me about third grade.

On the last day of school, she gave us cupcakes with sprinkles and little beach umbrellas and said have a super-duper summer and she'd wave to us in the hallway next year. She said third grade would be even more fun than second grade. She said we'd read bigger books and keep our old friends and make new ones and even get to be in the school play.

None of it is true. Because Veronica Grace Smithers has stolen my best friend and taken over recess. I'd call Veronica Grace Princess Bossy-Pants if I were allowed to call people names.

But I'm not.

So I won't.

Even though Veronica Grace is leaning over into my space and wrinkling her nose at my handwriting paper. "You make your cursive *E*s funny."

She holds up her paper. Her cursive *E* is loopy and swirly like it's supposed to be. Mine looks like a dog's been chewing on it, even though I really took my time. That is so not fair.

"All right, class. Listen up!" Mrs. Aloi shakes her maracas. "It's time for the most exciting part of our day. Marty, please collect everyone's papers, and then I'll have a big announcement."

I collect the papers super fast and hurry back to my seat to wait for Mrs. Aloi's big announcement. It must be huge news if it's going to be the most exciting part of our day.

"It's just about time for recess, but I know you've all been waiting to hear what the third-grade play will be," she says. "It's coming up in three weeks, so we'll be very busy getting ready. We will be practicing every day. This year, we've decided to perform our own version of an old fairy tale called *The Frog Prince.*"

"Is there dancing?" asks Kimmy Butler.

"Do we *have* to be in it?" asks Rupert Wingfield.

"Can I be the princess?" asks Veronica Grace Smithers.

"Can I, too?" asks Isabel Pike.

"Do we get to build props and stuff?" asks Alex Farley.

"Can I be the king?" asks Rasheena Wells.

"Can I do sound effects?" asks Jimmy Lawson. "I can burp so it sounds like a ribbit."

Mrs. Aloi shakes her maracas again. She says it's to remind us to listen, but I think she just likes shaking them. "We'll talk about all of that after recess. For now, just get thinking about kings and queens and castles, and get ready to have some out-of-your-seat fun."

I line up for recess, all excited. Out of my seat is my favorite place to be. Then I remember Mrs. Kramer's promise about third grade and that teachers have weird ideas about what's fun.

“Line up, everyone!” Veronica Grace shouts once we’re outside. She flips her hair back and forth while she waits. Veronica Grace likes her hair.

Even I can understand why. It's silky and smooth and the color of a yellow Lab, my favorite kind of dog. My hair is not silky or smooth. It's all thick and sticky-uppy and the color of pond mud.

"Are we all lined up?" Veronica Grace fluffs up her skirt. She's wearing a flower-pink churchy dress with glitter leggings and shiny black shoes.

"She looks like a movie star," Kimmy Butler whispers from her spot in line. Kimmy has black hair in pigtails and is the kind of girl who is always eating a cupcake. If she's not eating a cupcake, she has chocolate frosting smeared on her face because she just finished one, or she's looking around to see if somebody brought in birthday treats. And she's as bossy as Veronica Grace. I'd call Kimmy Frosting-Face Messy-Mouth if I were allowed to call people names.

But I'm not.

So I won't.

"We're going to practice for the big class play," Veronica Grace says.

"But we don't know the parts yet," I say.

"That's okay," Kimmy says. "We can dance. My big sister — she's in fifth grade — and she told me the third-grade play is always a fairy-tale sort of thing and there's always a prince and a princess and king and queen. And usually talking animals and magic spells. And sometimes ogres but not all the time. And there's always dancing."

"Perfect," Veronica Grace says. "We'll practice the dancing. There *has* to be dancing."

The other girls nod like it's a rule. There *has* to be dancing.

Even my best friend, Annie, nods. No, wait. Annie *used to* be my best friend. She *used to* catch crayfish and climb trees. She *used to* play in the woods behind her house with me, and

we'd pretend to be Jane Goodall, who is an amazing scientist who travels to Africa to save the chimpanzees in Tanzania. Annie and I *used to* pretend to save chimpanzees by the creek out back. *Now* she takes dancing lessons and curtsies and likes sparkly Veronica Grace better than me.

"Let's pretend we're at a fancy royal ball," Veronica Grace says. "I'll be a princess getting ready for my wedding. You can be princesses, too." Veronica Grace points to Kimmy Butler and Isabel Pike.

"We'll be the only princesses, right?" says Isabel. She has sparkly red sneakers that she uses to follow Veronica Grace everywhere. Even the bathroom. If I were allowed to call people names, I'd call Isabel Brainless, Sparkly Footed Sheep.

"The rest of you can be ladies-in-waiting," Veronica Grace says. "Mrs. Aloi said I could bring the dress-up box outside. Come get a gown."

"I don't really like playing dress-up," I say, "so I think I'll just —"

"Here!" Veronica Grace tosses me a slippery, shimmery, silver shirt and a tiara. "Put these on."

"No, thanks," I say, but Annie tugs my sleeve.

"Come on, it will be fun." She smiles at me, and I think maybe if I'm a good sport about dancing, she'll go with me to catch tadpoles later. Mom told me Annie's probably just getting to be friends with Veronica Grace because they're in dance class together now. She said if I'm patient, Annie will come back.

I hope so.

I look around. Everyone else is pulling on poofy, floofy pink dresses. Blech. The silver thing is better than a dress, so I put it on.

"Now make three lines over there," Veronica Grace says, and points to the crazy big sandbox the custodian, Mr. Klein, built for us.

We make three lines. Because Veronica Grace is like that.

Recess was more fun before Veronica Grace put herself in charge.

chapter 2

"Our first dance step will be the waltz," Veronica Grace says. "I saw it on *Ballroom of the Stars*, so I know exactly how it goes. Do this." She takes one big step, then two little steps. "One . . . two-three . . . one . . . two-three . . ."

Veronica Grace steps and twirls in her fluffy princess gown. All the girls one-two-three-step around after her. Except for Rasheena, who didn't want to be a princess *or* a lady-in-waiting. She offered to be the king, but Veronica Grace said no, so Rasheena left to play basketball with the fourth-grade boys. They look like they're having fun.

But Annie's still here one-two-three-stepping, so I try it, too.

Waltzing is hard. I keep tripping. Pretty soon, I hear boy shouts coming from the pond.

Boy shouts from the pond mean one of two things.

One — somebody pushed somebody else into the muddy stuff that is like quicksand and will suck your feet off if you're not careful.

Or two — somebody found something good.

Annie's looking over at the pond, too, and stumbles into the edge of the sandbox.

"No, no, no!" Veronica Grace shouts. "Watch *me.*" She moves over next to Annie to demonstrate again, and Annie falls back into line.

While Veronica Grace is busy, I sneak away to the pond.

"Whatcha got?" I ask Rupert Wingfield. Rupert wears an Orchard Street Otters shirt to school every day. Today, it is streaked with mud.

"Nothin' yet," Rupert says. He points to the water. Alex Farley is balanced on a rotten log. He hikes up the tool belt he always wears, leans over with one foot in the air behind him, and reaches out with his arm stretched so far it looks like it might stretch right off and splash into the pond. Finally, he puts his foot down and hops back onto the grass.

"Nope," he says. "Can't reach him."

"Who?" I ask.

"The fattest bullfrog in the whole universe," Jimmy Lawson says with a sigh.

I step onto the log. I look into the green-brown water. Beady frog eyes stare up at me. He's huge all right. But he's not out *that* far.

"I think I can get him." I roll up my jeans and push my slippery, shimmery, silver sleeves up to my elbows. I look back at the dancing lesson.

"No! No! No!" Veronica Grace yells from the sandbox. "It's one . . . TWO-three . . . one . . . TWO-three . . ."

I take one . . . two-three . . . four little steps to the end of the log. I lean down. I stretch out my slippery, shimmery arm.

The bullfrog blinks.

My fingers can almost tickle his webby toes.

I take a tiny shuffle step. I stretch a little more.

The bullfrog blinks again, and I hear a slow sucking noise.

At first, I think it's the frog. Then the sucking noise turns into a crazy big loud *SCHLOOP!* The other end of my log tips up out of the water, and I tumble toward the frog, face-first.

I close my hands around his cool, greeny smoothness right before my face splashes into the shallow, weedy water.

I sit up, but I can't wipe the pond slime off my face without letting go of the frog, and I'm sure not doing that after I went through all this trouble to catch him. Besides, the boys are waiting to see him.

I stand up, pull my sneakers one at a time from the shallow-water mud, and step back onto the grass. The boys gather around.

"Wow!" says Jimmy.

"Awesome!" says Alex. "He's the biggest bullfrog ever!"

He really is. Fat and slippery and fantastic. I don't even mind when he pees on my sleeve.

"Spectacular!" Rupert says, but he's looking at me — not the frog. "You're the coolest girl ever."

"Thanks," I say.

"Seriously, my sister would never catch a frog or even touch one. She says they're slimy and disgusting. I think you should be my sister instead."

I walk around the circle of boys so they can see the frog up close. Then I hear a bossy princess voice.

"What is *that*?" Veronica Grace has come over from the sandbox with a bunch of ladies-in-waiting following her. She stares at the frog like it's ten feet tall with two heads. "Gross!"

The ladies-in-waiting wrinkle their noses. Even Annie, who raised frogs with me from tadpoles last year, makes a yuck face.

Jane Goodall would never make a yuck face at a frog.

"Marty?"

It's the recess monitor, Mrs. Gardner. She's about a hundred years old and says she supervised George Washington on this playground, but we all know he's older than a hundred now.

I look down at my slippery, shimmery shirt. It's a mucky, muddy shirt now. And it's wet. With pond water and frog pee.

"Put the frog down, Marty. Then get inside to the nurse's office to change your clothes," Mrs. Gardner says.

I squat down at the edge of the pond, and the frog slips from between my fingers. One giant leap, and he's gone.

I wish I could do that.

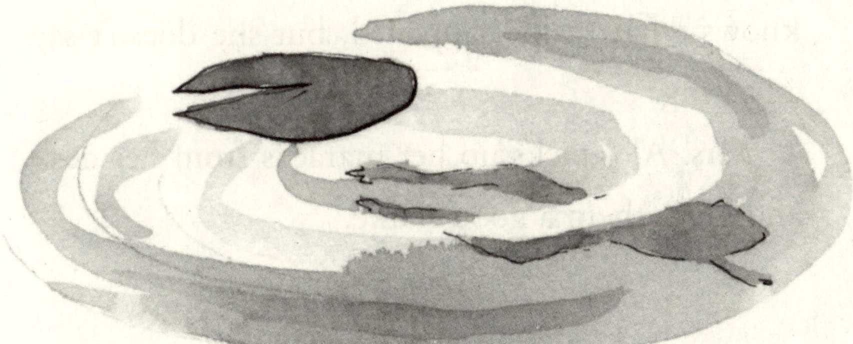

chapter 3

Everyone is doing the Mad Minute multiplication work sheet when I get back to the classroom. My muddy frog-pond jeans are wadded up in a plastic bag, and I'm wearing the nurse's emergency pants. They're too baggy and keep falling down in back, but that's not the worst part.

"She must have had an accident," Mary Beth Owens whispers to her friend Emma, just loud enough so I can hear. Emma nods and looks away from me. Annie's sitting right next to them and knows what really happened, but she doesn't say anything.

Mrs. Aloi picks up her maracas from her desk and gives them a good shake.

“Okay, class,” she says. “While you were at recess today, I put the finishing touches on the cast list for our play. We’ll practice every day starting tomorrow to get ready for the big show in three weeks.”

Veronica Grace waves her hand. "Mrs. Aloi, there's dancing, right? There *has* to be dancing. Will we have fancy costumes? Can I be a princess?"

"Can I be one, too?" Isabel asks.

"Can I, too?" Kimmy asks. She has her cupcake from lunch hidden in the bottom of her desk and keeps licking frosting off her fingers.

Mrs. Aloi holds up her hand. Everyone keeps talking until she shakes the maracas again.

"First, I want to tell you a little about the play," she says. "*The Frog Prince* is an old fairy tale from the Grimm Brothers. In the story, a beautiful princess goes walking in the woods . . ."

Veronica Grace sits up very straight.

". . . and she's playing with her golden ball, throwing it up and catching it again."

Veronica Grace tosses her eraser a few times and grins like she already has the part.

"But then she drops her golden ball, her very favorite toy, down a deep well. She sits at the edge of the well and cries."

Veronica Grace makes a sad face.

"A big fat frog comes up from the water and offers to help the princess if she'll take him back to the castle to live with her."

"Eww!" Veronica Grace says.

"That's what the princess thought, too," Mrs. Aloi says. "But she agreed because she really wanted her golden ball back. So the frog dove deep into the well and got it for her. And then he followed her back to the castle and went right up to her room to have supper with her."

Veronica Grace looks like she just found a frog in her lunch box.

"The princess was very mean to the frog and tried to send him away. But the king told her she needed to keep her promise and let the frog live with her. That night, the frog took a big leap onto the princess's beautiful bedspread and settled down on her pillow."

"Eww! Frogs are *so* disgusting. Eeewww!!" Veronica Grace says again.

Mrs. Aloi shakes her maracas. "Finally, the princess was so disgusted with the frog that she threw him against the wall. Actually, in one version of the story, she chops off his head, but we won't do that. So she threw him against the wall, and guess what?"

"He died?" Rupert says. I thought it was a pretty good guess, but Mrs. Aloi shakes her head.

"He turned into a handsome prince and married the princess and they lived happily ever after."

We all stare at her.

"She threw him against the wall?" Rupert asks again. Mrs. Aloi nods. "And he didn't die and then he married her?"

"It's a fairy tale, Rupert."

"She marries him even though he used to be a

frog?" Veronica Grace's mouth and nose are all scrunched up. Mrs. Aloi nods.

"Mrs. Aloi, I cannot possibly be that princess. I'm afraid I won't be able to star in the show after all," Veronica Grace says sadly.

Mrs. Aloi smiles. "That's fine, because I don't have you cast for that part anyway. You're going to be the queen, Veronica Grace. Rupert will be the prince. Let's see . . . Rasheena, you asked if you could be the king, right?" Rasheena nods. "Rasheena's the king. Annie, Kimmy, Isabel, Jimmy, and Alex, you're forest animals. And our frog princess . . ." She looks down at her list. ". . . will be Marty McGuire."

chapter 4

I'm not doing it.

I tell Mrs. Aloi at the end of the day. I'll help paint scenery instead. I don't do princess things.

"You'd be so good at it," she says.

"Sorry."

The bell rings, and I pick up my backpack.

"We'll talk tomorrow," Mrs. Aloi says. I wave and walk out. We can talk, but it won't matter. Let Veronica Grace or Kimmy or Isabel or their new friend Annie dance around in some frilly, floofy costume. I am *not* being the princess.

Mom's already waiting, so I open the car door and plop my backpack down on the seat next to me.

"Marty?"

"Hi, Mom."

"Why are you wearing the emergency clothes from the nurse again?" she asks.

"What do you mean 'again'?"

"You borrowed the emergency clothes last Tuesday when you ripped your pants trying to climb the oak tree outside the art room because you were chasing that squirrel so you could try to feed him your leftover granola bar."

Oh. That.

"I wasn't actually chasing the squirrel. I saw him *after* I got up there and thought he looked hungry. I climbed the tree because the kickball got stuck."

"Mm-hm."

"Because Mark Pignati always kicks it too high."

"Mm-hm."

"They really shouldn't let fourth graders play."

"Marty?"

"Yes?"

"Why are you wearing the emergency clothes *today*?"

Oh. That.

"Mostly because of the frog pee, I guess."

Mom raises one eyebrow. I look in the rearview

mirror and try to raise mine back at her, but I can't. That is so not fair.

"We'll have a little talk about this at dinner," she says.

When we pull into the driveway, Dad is just getting out of his car. His *Learning Is FUN!* bag is full of fifth-grade papers. He'll grade them while he watches the Boston Red Sox

play on TV tonight. He reaches for the door handle but stops and stares into the house through the window.

"Uh-oh," Mom says, and climbs out of the car.

"Sparky's out again," Dad says. "Sorry, Rachel. I'd help, but she clawed a hole in my good school pants last time." He sits down on the steps and pulls out a stack of papers to grade. Mom opens the screen door and slips inside.

"Wait here," she says.

Sparky is our raccoon. She's not our raccoon, actually. She's God's raccoon. That's what Mom says. But we're taking care of her until her paw is healed.

Her paw needs healing because she got into the McCormicks' attic last week. Mr. McCormick tried to trap her under a laundry basket and caught her paw under the edge.

Mrs. McCormick says the raccoon threw a fit, screaming and scratching and clawing, with her teeth all pointy and everything. And then Mr. McCormick didn't know what to do because he had that wild crazy raccoon under the laundry basket, so he sat down on the basket and sent Mrs. McCormick to get Mom.

My mom is a wildlife rehabilitator. She helps animals that are hurt and sometimes comes to get them out of your attic if you have them trapped and are sitting on a laundry basket on top of them.

But Mom wasn't home. So Mr. McCormick sat on the laundry basket for two hours. He says Mrs. McCormick brought him a nice glass of lemonade and his crossword puzzle, so it wasn't so bad except for the raccoon flopping all around under his behind.

That's why we have Sparky.

Sparky is supposed to live in her cage on the porch.

But it doesn't always work out that way.

Like now. When I peek in through the screen door, I can see Sparky on top of the refrigerator with her front paws in a package of Fig Newtons.

"Here, baby . . ." Mom says. Sparky hisses and whips a Fig Newton at Mom's head. Then Sparky backs her bottom under the cupboard. I hope she doesn't get stuck under there. She has a pretty big bottom.

Mom reaches down to get the noose.

"It's okay, baby. You'll be okay. . . ." As Mom talks, she moves the noose closer to Sparky's bottom. She taps the refrigerator near Sparky's head to make her back up. Sparky backs herself right into Mom's trap.

When Mom catches her, Sparky goes crazy.

She screams bad words in raccoon language. She reminds me of the babysitter we had from Russia that time.

Mom stuffs Sparky in her cage and slams the door shut.

"There," she says. "Now, Marty, about those emergency clothes . . ."

chapter 5

We have a little talk at dinner.

"A little talk" is when you explain why you went in the pond after the frog. My mother traps fat-bottomed raccoons for a job. You'd think she would understand this kind of thing.

She doesn't. She sends me to my room. And I have to finish my peas first.

That is so not fair.

I'm telling all this to Bob the Lion when the phone rings. Bob is the best stuffed animal ever. Mrs. McCormick gave him to me when I was born. He has always been a great listener.

Mom answers the phone. Bob and I hold our ears to the door.

"Well, hello, Mrs. Aloi," Mom says. This is not good.

"The Frog Prince?" Mom says to the phone. "Oh, how marvelous! Oh, the princess? That's fantastic!"

Bob the Lion looks up at me. I shake my head. "I'm not doing it," I whisper to him.

"She said no?" Mom says. "I can't imagine why. . . . Oh, I see. . . . No, she does not like dresses, but I'm sure we'll work it out. . . . Uh-huh. . . . Well, yes, I'll talk with her, and I think you can count on Princess Marty reporting for duty tomorrow. Okay. . . . Uh-huh. . . . You have a good night, too. Bye."

I drop Bob and step back from my door just as Mom opens it.

"Marty, that was Mrs. Aloi. She says you're going to be the lead in your third-grade play."

"She must have dialed the wrong number."

"Marty . . ."

"Mom, it's a princess part. I'm not a princessy girl."

"Marty, it's such a fun opportunity."

"To wear a stupid frilly dress?"

"Well, maybe you won't have to wear —"

"I know I won't have to because I'm not doing it."

"Marty . . ." Mom picks Bob up from the carpet and pets his mane. He used to be prettier and softer before I threw up on him two years ago. We had to put him through the wash, and his mane has been all crazy frizzy big since he came out of the dryer.

"Nope." I take Bob back and put him on my pillow.

"But Mrs. Aloi will be so disappointed."

"She can get Veronica Grace. Or Kimmy. Or Isabel. Or Annie. Annie's all princessy now, too. She didn't come back like you said."

"Give her time, Marty. She's just trying something new. It's good to make friends and try out lots of different things." Mom looks down at my muddy pants in the plastic accident bag from the nurse. "And for now, I think a little princess practice would be good for you. I told Mrs. Aloi you're going to do it."

"But, Mom —"

"But nothing. You're going to go to school tomorrow and report for princess duty." She picks up the muddy frog clothes and leaves.

"This is so not fair," I tell Bob.

Bob understands. He doesn't like fancy pink dresses either.

chapter 6

Play practice isn't until the end of the school day, but it feels like the play has taken over everything.

Reading time. We have to read *The Frog Prince* and then pretend we're the frog writing a diary entry about what happened at the well.

Jimmy Lawson raises his hand. "Mrs. Aloi?"

"Yes?"

"Frogs can't write on account of their webbed feet, so how about we just tell you what we'd write if we could write, even though we can't?"

"No. You're already pretending to be frogs. Pretend to be magical frogs who can write."

"I'll be a magical frog and cast a spell so it's already done," Jimmy whispers. He waves his pencil like a wand, but nothing happens, so he starts writing the regular way.

Math time. If there are twenty flies buzzing around the well, and the frog eats seven of them, how many flies are left?

Jimmy Lawson raises his hand. "None."

"None?" Mrs. Aloi raises her eyebrows. "Look at the picture again, Jimmy. Twenty flies . . . and just seven get eaten."

"Yeah, but do you really think they're just going to sit there when all their friends keep getting sucked up on a big old frog tongue? They'd leave. So there are none."

Gym class. The boys get to hop like frogs around the gym. The girls are supposed to dance and twirl like princesses in the opposite direction. I ask if I can be a frog instead of a princess. Mr. Miller says no, I'll be fine as a princess. I'm not fine. I get so dizzy twirling that I trip over one of Isabel's sparkly sneakers and fall down. Then Rupert frog-hops right onto my pinkie finger while I'm trying to get up. Annie tries to help me up, but I don't let her. I ask to go to the nurse and get an ice pack, but Mr. Miller says I'll be fine. Sure. No one frog-hopped on his pinkie finger.

Lunch. Everybody talks about the play. Veronica Grace takes a bite of her peanut butter and jelly sandwich on white bread with the crust cut off and says, "Thank goodness I'm the queen instead of the princess and I don't have to handle a filthy frog."

I have nothing to be thankful for. I have tuna fish instead of peanut butter and jelly. It is on wheat bread, with crust. I am the princess, even though I don't do princesses. That is so not fair.

Science. We learn about frog anatomy. That's a fancy way of saying "frog parts." Like their eardrums that are round spots on the sides of their heads. I already knew about that because Mom taught me all about bullfrogs on our camping trip to Collins Pond last year. The only part I didn't know is that you can look at the eardrum to tell if you have a boy frog or a girl frog. If the eardrum is about the size of the frog's eye, then it's a girl frog. If the eardrum is about twice as big as the frog's eye, then it's a boy frog. I wonder if that huge frog at the pond is a boy or a girl.

The Frog
EYE
EAR DRUM
NOSTRILS
MOUTH
THIGH
UPPER ARM
HANDS
ANKLE
FOOT
FOREARM
WEBBED TOES
KNEE
HB

Art class. We can't work on our class mural today because we have to make scenery. Jimmy, Rupert, and I wrap paper around one of the big cafeteria garbage cans and paint it to make it look like a wishing well. It looks pretty good. It still smells like cafeteria peas, though.

Music class. Mrs. Campbell plays the piano and we sing. There's a song about the Frog Prince, too. Who knew?

After music class, we have fifteen minutes of quiet seatwork time before we practice the play. Even quiet seatwork sounds better than being a princess, so I take out my math problems. But pretty soon there's a tap on my shoulder.

"Marty, could I talk to you in the hall for a minute?"

"Me?" My stomach does a little flip.

"Don't worry, you're not in trouble," Mrs. Aloi whispers. "I just want to talk to you."

I follow her down my row of desks, past six pairs of eyes that look at me like I'm in trouble even though she says I'm not, and step out into the hall.

"I'm glad you decided you'd be the princess," she says.

"I didn't. It got decided for me when you called my parents." If I were allowed to call people names, I'd call Mrs. Aloi Princess-Pushing Tattle-Tale right now.

But I'm not.

So I don't. Especially since she's a teacher and everything.

Mrs. Aloi sighs. "Do you know why I chose you to be the princess?"

"To punish me for falling in the pond?"

"No, no, no. Marty, it's an honor to have the lead in the play. That's a job that can be done only by somebody with a lot of talent and confidence. Somebody with a strong voice and lots of energy. Somebody brave and smart who can think on her feet. You're perfect, Marty. You'll be so good at this if you give it a try."

EXIT

Now I feel bad about wishing I could call her that tattler name. I turn away and look through the window of the classroom door. I watch Jimmy Lawson fold his math assignment into an airplane and launch it into the reading area, and I think about what she said.

Me? Brave and smart? With talent and confidence and energy? Well, the last part I knew because Mom always complains I have too much. But still . . .

"Marty?" Mrs. Aloi's still looking at me. "Are you game to at least give it a try?"

I nod. "Okay." And I open the door and head back to my desk.

She sounds like she's really counting on me. And after all, it's only two weeks. In two weeks, I'll never have to dress up like a princess again.

"All right, class. It's finally time to practice the play." Mrs. Aloi gives her maracas a good shake. "We have a special guest joining us for play practice. James Jackson is a theater professor at the college, and he's going to be helping us out with our acting skills."

"Does he work with the big kids?" Jimmy asks.

"He works with college students and acts in plays, too. How many of you went to see *Cinderella* at the downtown stage last summer?"

We all raise our hands.

"Remember the prince?"

We nod. He was just about the greatest prince ever, the way he danced all over and whisked Cinderella away from those evil stepsisters.

"That was Mr. Jackson. Until he gets here, we'll start working on the dance in the first scene of the show." Mrs. Aloi puts us in three lines. "It's going to be a waltz. Veronica Grace told me you've been practicing that."

"Well . . ." Veronica Grace looks at me. "*Some* of us have."

"Hey, wait," Jimmy Lawson says. "I'm not a prince or anything. I'm just one of the squirrels in the forest, so I wouldn't waltz."

"No, you waltz, too," Mrs. Aloi says. "You can pretend to be a magical squirrel who knows how to waltz. Let's go."

chapter 7

Jimmy waltzes — along with the rest of us — for almost half an hour, until we know the first scene. It's a dance with the princess and king and queen and all the animals of the forest, including Isabel the owl, Annie the bluebird, Kimmy the frosting-face chipmunk, and Jimmy the magical dancing squirrel.

Then everyone leaves the stage, and I stand next to the garbage can that looks like a wishing well and smells like peas. My lines are taped to the side of the garbage can on note cards now, but they won't be there once I memorize them. I play with my golden ball.

"Hold on," Mrs. Aloi says. "Could you act like you really like that ball, Marty? It's made of gold, you know."

I look down at the ball in my hand. It's one of those bouncy Super Balls you get out of gumball machines at the grocery store if your mother gives you a quarter. It smells like dirty rubber and is more greenish than golden. It's also a little sticky.

But I have a great imagination. That's what Mom says. So I imagine it's really gold. I look at it like it's my favorite toy ever, even better than Bob the Lion.

I toss it in the garbage can and try to look sad.

"Remember," Mrs. Aloi says. "It was your favorite! And it's gone."

Isabel raises her hand. "I think the princess would cry if she lost her favorite toy."

"Great idea." Mrs. Aloi turns to me. "Try to cry this time."

"Okay . . . I'll try." I bend down into the garbage can, which it turns out smells like peas because there *are* smushed peas in the bottom, and get the ball. I toss it in again and imagine

Bob the Lion disappearing forever into a sea of smelly smushed peas. It almost makes me cry a little.

"Better!" Mrs. Aloi says. "Now the frog comes up from the well."

I peek into the garbage can. It's empty except for the ball and the peas.

"Oh," Mrs. Aloi says. "I guess I forgot the frog." She pulls a frog stuffed animal with long floppy legs out of her desk drawer. It's the sort of

stuffed animal you win at the county fair if you can't pop the balloon with the dart but you get a prize for trying.

"That's it?" I say. "That's not a bullfrog." It looks like a frog that a four-year-old would draw. Its eyes are all buggy and huge and white, and its legs are too skinny, and it's all the wrong colors — a way-too-fuzzy neon green with purple spots.

"It will be just fine," Mrs. Aloi says. "Now where's our prince?"

"Right here." Rupert Wingfield steps forward. He told me at recess he didn't want to be the prince any more than I want to be the princess, but his parents are making him do it, too.

"Get in the garbage can," Mrs. Aloi says.

"Get *in* it?"

"Yes."

"But it smells like peas in there."

She points. Rupert climbs in, and she hands him the frog. "Now, when you hear the princess

crying, make the frog pop up and say, 'How can I help you, fair princess?' "

Rupert ducks down into the garbage can, but before I can toss the ball in after him, the classroom door opens again, and a tall guy walks in.

"Sorry I'm late," he says, and smiles so big that I can see every one of his bright white teeth.

"I'm James Jackson, and I'm happy to be working with you fine actors and actresses. You must be our princess." He reaches out to shake my hand. His head is perfectly bald, and he's way cooler than any teacher I've ever met. "So where are we?" he asks.

"I'm about to lose this." I hold up the bouncy ball. "And then I'll cry and Rupert will pop up from the garbage can and ask if he can help."

"Let's get one thing straight right now," James says. He smiles a huge smile and rests his hand on the edge of the garbage can. "We're going to make magic here. Theater is magic. So this can never be a garbage can again. It's an enchanted wishing well." He runs his hand over our painted-on cobblestones. "It's made of cool, damp, mossy old stones, full of ancient magic. Anything can happen here." When I look at his face, all serious and believing, I believe it, too. I can't even smell the peas anymore.

“What I meant,” I say, “was that I’m about to lose my golden ball.” I hold it up and stare at it in the classroom light. I imagine it sparkling in my hand, and I sniffle a little. “It’s my favorite thing, and I don’t know what I’ll do without it.”

“That’s the magic!” James says. “Now let’s go for it.”

chapter 8

We practice our lines every morning, and James helps run our rehearsal at the end of every school day.

On the first Friday, he teaches us how to improvise. That's a fancy word for making stuff up when you can't remember a line or you forget what you're supposed to do.

"Improvisation is the art of being spontaneous," James says.

"What's 'spontaneous'?" Rupert asks.

"It's when you do or say something without thinking about it. You just do it." He snaps his fingers.

"Hey!" Jimmy Lawson says. "I'm going to be good at this. My mom says I never think before I say stuff."

"Let's give it a try with a fun game, okay? It's called Sculpture Garden. Anybody know what a sculpture garden is?"

Annie raises her hand. "It's a collection of statues. My mom and dad took me to the Beverly Cleary Sculpture Garden in Oregon when we went there to visit my aunt. There's a statue of Henry Huggins and one of his dog Ribsy and one of Ramona Quimby stomping in a puddle."

"Great," James says. "We're going to be a collection of statues, too. And all those statues will work together to tell a story. Ready to play?" We nod, and James lines up the first group and has us count off from one to eight. "Now, who's number one?"

Veronica Grace raises her hand.

"You're the first statue," James tells her. "Stand in the center of the room, strike a pose, and announce who you are and what you're doing.

Like, if you were that statue Annie told us about, you'd say, 'I'm Ramona, and I'm splashing in a puddle.'"

"Okay." Veronica Grace thinks for a second. Then she skips to the center of the room and starts twirling around in circles. "I'm a beautiful princess dancing at my wedding."

"Okay, but you have to stand perfectly still in one pose," James says, "like you're frozen. Sculptures don't twirl."

Veronica Grace frowns, but she freezes up on her tiptoes with her arms in a circle over her head.

"Great," James says. "Now whoever is number two goes up and adds to the sculpture garden."

"That's me," Annie says. She scrunches up small under one of the desks right next to Veronica Grace's princess statue and says, "I'm a mouse that snuck into the castle, and I'm scurrying under the table looking for crumbs of wedding cake."

"You're adding to the story. That's great!" James says.

"No, it's not!" Veronica Grace unfreezes. She puts her princess hands on her hips. "You can't be a mouse at my wedding."

"Yes, I can," says Annie. "I'm improvising."

"Exactly," James says. "One of the rules of improvising is that everyone's ideas are valued. When one of your fellow actors or actresses makes a decision to improvise, you can't question. You just have to go with the idea, and build on it." He looks at Veronica Grace. She gets back up on her tiptoes but doesn't look happy about it. She keeps making faces at Annie-mouse-statue under the desk.

"Number three?"

Jimmy Lawson walks to the desk Annie's under and curls up into an even tinier ball next to her. "I'm one of the cake crumbs," he says.

James laughs and nods. "Now you've got it. Keep going."

Rasheena steps up, holds her head high, grabs a yardstick, and raises it like a sword. "I'm the king, calling for order in the court!"

Rupert gets down on his hands and knees in a ready-to-pounce position. "I'm the cat sniffing out the mouse who's sniffing out the cake crumbs." Annie-mouse-statue looks nervous, but she stays still.

Kimmy Butler and Isabel Pike climb up onto the desks, pretending to be wedding guests who saw the mouse and got scared. That makes Mrs. Aloi tap her fingers on her desk because no one is allowed to climb on the desks, ever, but James doesn't know that and doesn't look like he cares, so he just keeps going.

"Number eight?"

It's my turn, and I've been having so much fun watching, I forgot to think of something to do. Finally, I grab a purple pillow from the reading area, drop it in the center of the scene, and do a headstand on it. "I'm the court jester. I'm providing the entertainment."

"Fantastic," James says. "Now hold that scene a minute and really think about getting into character. Be that princess. That cat. That . . . cake crumb." Jimmy Lawson scrunches smaller.

I try to be perfectly still and think court jester thoughts, but all the blood is rushing to my head and making me see things all spotty, so I'm wobbling a little. I'm pretty sure that's bad because statues don't wobble unless they're about to fall down.

Just in time, James says, "Now, when I clap my hands, the sculpture garden comes to life. I want you to do — and say — whatever your character would do and say in this situation, given everything happening on our stage right now. Ready?"

James claps his hands and I let my feet drop. When I stand up, I forget about being the court jester for a minute because Annie-mouse is scampering around on her hands and knees, chasing after Jimmy the crumb, who is rolling from desk to desk. Rupert-cat is chasing Annie, and Rasheena is waving her sword, shouting, "Halt! Stop that! In the name of the king!"

Veronica Grace must be a great actress because she looks just as bug-eyed as she would if Annie were a real mouse. She jumps up on the desks with Kimmy and Isabel to get out of the way.

I remember then I'm supposed to be entertaining them all, and so even though they're kind of busy, I do a cartwheel. But when I land, Jimmy the crumb is rolling under me, so I fall on him, and Annie crashes into us.

"I declare this wedding finished!" Rasheena yells. And she yells it in such a big booming voice that we all just stare for a minute.

"What is going on here?" Mrs. Grimes is

standing in the door. In all the wedding excitement, no one even heard her clickety-clackety shoes coming.

"I — we — uhh . . ." Mrs. Aloi points to James.

"Just a little drama activity," he says. "We're getting them ready for the big play next week."

Mrs. Aloi looks scared that *she* might get sent to the office, but Mrs. Grimes just nods once, says, "Must be *some* play," and leaves. This time, we hear her shoes clickety-clacking all the way back to her office.

"You heard her," James says. "It's going to be some play. Let's get to work."

chapter 9

By the second Friday of rehearsals, I'm really good at losing my golden ball. I almost cry every time. And I haven't called the wishing well a garbage can in three days.

"One week to your big day, and you're almost ready," James says. "Let's move on to the scene in the castle. Okay, princess. You've made this deal with the frog, and you really, really regret it. You can't stand the frog. Let's see it."

I sit down in the chair where I'm supposed to be having my royal dinner and stare at the stuffed frog next to me. I try to look like I can't stand him, but he's very cute and froggy in a silly, ugly sort of way.

"Marty, try again." Mrs. Aloi rushes in

and scoops up the frog. "This is a horrible, slimy, disgusting creature. You have to look disgusted."

I try again. Mostly I just feel bad for it, though.

James takes the frog from her and squats down next to me. "Here's the thing," he says. "You're looking at this frog like Marty would look at it, right?"

I nod.

"And I'm going to guess that Marty really likes frogs?"

I nod again.

James gives me the big white smile. "I like frogs, too," he says. "Did you know some frogs can jump up to twenty times the length of their bodies? That would be like me jumping more than a hundred feet!"

It's my turn to smile. "Yep, and did *you* know

the longest frog jump ever was made by a frog named Santjie in South Africa?"

Annie steps up and tugs my sleeve. "Hey—yeah! We read about him at the frog exhibit at the Museum of Natural History. The frog went almost thirty-three and a half feet in just three jumps!"

It was really awesome.

For a minute, I forget I'm mad at Annie. She and James and I start frog-hopping around the room. We have a great time until we hear the maracas.

"Have we forgotten who is the princess and who is the frog?" Mrs. Aloi puts her hands on her hips.

"Just a little character exploration." James takes my hand and pulls me up to stand. Annie goes back to her tree in the forest. "So," James says, "*Marty* loves frogs. But . . ."

"But I'm not Marty."

"Right," he says, and tips my chin up into the air. "Get some finicky princess attitude going. Let's try it again."

When I think about it that way, it's kind of fun. I imagine I'm even snootier and snippier and fancier than Veronica Grace. I narrow my eyes and wrinkle my nose up at that frog on the chair next to me.

"Perfect!" James says.

Finally, the frog ends up on my pillow. I said I'd let him share my bed, but I'm supposed to throw him against the wall instead. Then the frog is supposed to turn into the prince.

"Be gone with you!" I yell. I hold the frog by one of its long dangly legs and whirl it

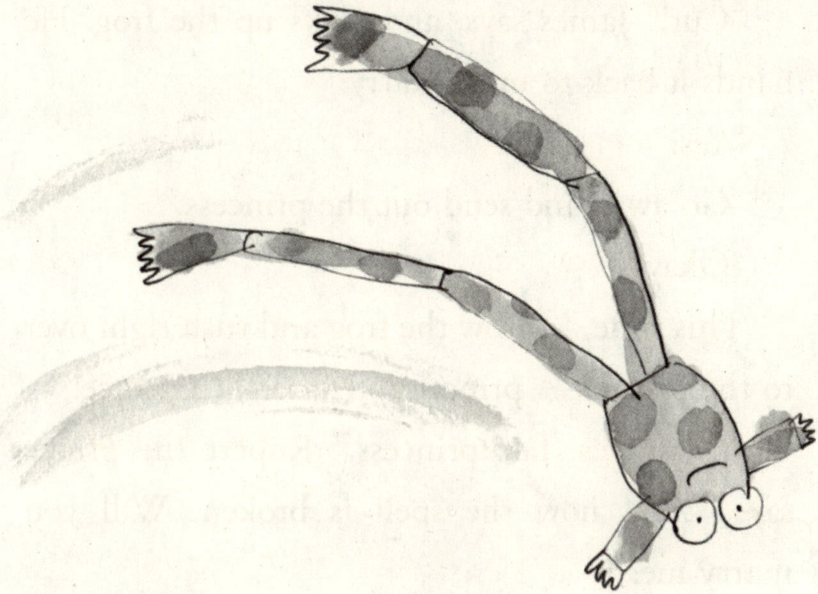

round and round in circles over my head before I let go. The stuffed frog flops against the classroom wall and lands under the chalkboard in a pile of dust.

Rupert steps out from behind the bookshelf with his crown on. The princess is supposed to be very happy to see him. I'm not happy. I feel bad for the stuffed frog.

"Cut!" James says, and picks up the frog. He hands it back to me. "Marty?"

"Yes?"

"Go away and send out the princess."

"Okay."

This time, I throw the frog and rush right over to the prince. "A prince! You're really a prince!"

"Why, yes, fair princess," Rupert the prince says. "And now the spell is broken. Will you marry me?"

"Of course!" I say, and we link arms and walk offstage while my parents, the queen and king, smile and wave.

"Better?" I ask.

James applauds. "Perfect."

"Okay, but there's still something I don't get," I say.

"What's that?"

"Well, the princess can't stand the frog, right? I mean, she hates it and ends up throwing it against a wall, and then when she finds out it was really a prince, she loves him."

"Right," James says.

"And you expect him to be okay with that?" I point to Rupert.

"My feelings *were* kind of hurt," he says.

"I know, I know," James says. "But you have to remember this story was written a long time ago."

Annie jumps in again. "Actually, my mom told me that in a newer version of the fairy tale, the princess doesn't throw the frog against the wall or cut its head off or anything awful like that. She kisses it, and sees that it's really beautiful, and that's what breaks the spell."

"See, that makes more sense," I say.

"Ewww!" Veronica Grace squeals.

"Oh, be quiet." I look down at the stuffed frog in my hands. He looks sad about the whole thing. His mouth is too small, and his eyes are too big,

and he doesn't even have any eardrums. He has a beanbag bottom that's all droopy. He'd never survive in a real pond.

I toss him to Rupert.

"Ribbit!" Rupert says, and makes the frog jump onto Veronica Grace's desk.

She screams.

"Ha! Imagine if it were a real frog," I say.

And then I get a great idea. It's not a princess idea at all. It's a one-hundred percent Marty idea.

I look over at Rupert, and before I can say a word, he's smiling like crazy.

"Are you thinking what I'm thinking?" I ask.

He nods. "I sure am."

Turns out my Marty idea is a Rupert idea, too.

And it's the best idea ever.

chapter 10

"You're late." On Friday, the morning of our play, Rupert's sitting on the school fence with his father's long-handled fishing net leaning next to him. "School starts in fifteen minutes. I thought you weren't coming."

"Sorry. Sparky got out of her cage again, and when we opened the kitchen door to leave, she came flying in and knocked over the garbage can, and there were chicken bones and potato peels all over the kitchen floor, and Mom made me clean up while she went to find Sparky."

"Oh." Rupert hops down and picks up the net. "Did she get her?"

"Yeah, but it took awhile. She was tucked up on the top shelf of Mom's closet, and it's all scrunchy tight up there, so it was hard to reach her with the noose, and then she got mad and started throwing shoes down at Mom, and one hit her in the head so I had to go get her ice for it." I start walking with him toward the pond. "I remembered the aquarium, though."

I hold up the little plastic aquarium we used to keep my goldfish in before they died. Rupert called me on the phone three times last night to make sure I didn't forget it. Mom kept asking what was going on. "Are you and Annie going to look for crayfish?"

"Nope. Annie doesn't care about that stuff anymore. This is . . . um . . . for a school project."

And it is. Kind of.

"Do you really think it will work?" Rupert asks.

"Definitely. It's perfect."

We hide the net and aquarium in the tall grass right next to the pond before we go to our classroom.

"Remember," Rupert whispers as we hang up our jackets in our cubbies. "Act normal at recess, and play with the girls and stuff. And then at twelve twenty-five . . ." We both look at our watches. We set them to the exact same perfect time this morning. ". . . meet me by the pond and we'll get the net and catch him."

"Or her," I say.

"I'm pretty sure it's a him," he says.

"Did you check the eardrums?"

"What?"

"Never mind, I'll show you later."

I try to concentrate on schoolwork, but

it's hard. Everyone's practically bursting with play talk.

"Are your parents coming?"

"Is somebody going to fix our hair tonight?"

"Ohh, do we get makeup?!"

"Do we get to have snacks after the play?"

"What if I forget my part?"

Even Mrs. Aloi's maracas can't settle us down. Veronica Grace keeps sneaking back to the closet to check on her queen costume. She has a fit when she thinks her tiara is missing, but really it's just over on the shelf drying because Mrs. Aloi glued some extra jewels on it. The whole time I'm working on my math practice pages, I can hear Rupert whispering lines to himself behind me.

I try to pay attention to multiplication and division facts, but all I can think about is the big show tonight.

And the dress rehearsal this afternoon.

And how much I hope our plan will work.

And how I wish the morning would go by faster. But it doesn't.

Reading time. We hear another Frog Prince story and pretend we're newspaper reporters writing articles about the wedding. Jimmy Lawson asks if he can write the story of the princess beating up the frog instead. Mrs. Aloi says no.

Math time. If the princess tosses her ball ten times before she drops it in the well and then twelve times after the frog gives it back to her, how many times does she toss the ball altogether?

Jimmy Lawson raises his hand. "Just ten."

Mrs. Aloi frowns. "But then after the frog gives it back, Jimmy . . ."

"Do you really think she'd just go right back to playing with it?" Jimmy says. "I mean, she thinks the frog is all disgusting. She's not going to just take the ball out of its mouth and start playing with it again. It'd be all covered with frog spit."

"Ewwww!" says Veronica Grace.

Recess.

I slide down the slide.

I swing on the swings.

I play freeze tag.

I even help Annie and Isabel try to catch Jimmy Lawson so Isabel can kiss him. He's too fast, though, and I wasn't trying very hard anyway because that would be awful for Jimmy.

Finally, my watch says 12:25. It's almost time to head back inside, but just as everyone else starts lining up at the door, I zip over to the edge of the pond, where Rupert's waiting with the net and aquarium, all set up with water and rocks and plants.

"He's out! He's really out! And he's close this time! He's right there!" Rupert is so excited, his glasses are slipping off his nose and he's just letting them go. He leans way over with the net and just like that, he scoops up the biggest bullfrog ever.

The frog isn't flopping or jumping or anything. He's just looking up at us like he knows this is important and he ought to just go along with it.

Actually, no. Not he. She.

"Rupert! It's not a boy bullfrog — it's a girl. Look! The eardrum things are the same size as the eyes. It's a girl bullfrog!"

"Well, that's no good." Rupert frowns.

"Why not?"

"Because wouldn't a girl bullfrog turn into a princess instead of a prince?"

He has a point. But there's no time to talk about it now.

"Hey, whatcha doing?" Annie skips up to us and looks down. "Wow! He's huge. Are you bringing him inside? This is for the play, isn't it? Oh — it'll be so much better with a real frog. Can I help?"

"No," I say at the same time Rupert says, "Yeah."

Before we can argue, Mrs. Gardner calls again. "Third graders, inside NOW!" She starts walking our way.

"Here!" Annie quick takes off her sweater, wraps the frog in it, and gives it back to Rupert. She looks cold, but she's smiling. And she doesn't look prissy or princessy at all. She looks like plain old Annie.

"Thanks," I say. "We're going to hide her in the garbage can — I mean the wishing well — so she can be in the play instead of that dumb beanbag frog. Let's go talk to Mrs. Gardner so Rupert can get away."

Annie nods and picks up the aquarium while I grab the net. Rupert holds the frog in the sweater close to his chest and runs off toward the slides, where some other kids are trying to stay outside without being noticed.

"Hi, Mrs. Gardner," Annie says. "We had a question, so we came right to you."

"What's that, girls?"

"Do we go straight to the auditorium for practice today or back to class first?"

"Head right for the stage." Mrs. Gardner points to the door. "And get moving. You're late."

"Okay — thanks!"

We do go straight to the auditorium, but we go in the back doors, where all the props and scenery and stuff are stored.

"Rupert?" I whisper into the dark.

"Over here."

I find him and set down the aquarium so he can put in the frog. He pushes the aquarium behind a refrigerator box that the kindergartners painted to look like a candy store last spring. He hands Annie the frog sweater, and she puts it right back on.

Veronica Grace would never do that. Jane Goodall would, though. Maybe Mom was right about Annie.

"We better go," Rupert says.

I look back. "We'll visit after school," I promise the frog. "You'll be able to see the dress rehearsal from here. And tonight, you get your very own part in the show."

chapter 11

Dress rehearsal is perfect until the very end. Rupert is waiting to appear after I throw the stuffed frog against the wall. He looks pretty snazzy in his prince outfit, but I think he's nervous. He keeps bumping into everything and has almost knocked the wishing well over three times.

"Be gone with you!" I shout at the stuffed frog. I grab it by one webbed foot and whirl it in circles over my head, getting ready to throw it against the wall for what feels like the hundredth time.

But before I can let go, the frog goes flying in the wrong direction. It's missing one leg, which is still dangling in my hand, but it flies anyway. Out over the audience where Mrs. Sample's

first graders came to watch. They all jump up and try to catch it but then say, "Ow!" because little tiny frog-bottom beads are hitting them in the face. I hear billions of beads falling on the hard auditorium floor and rolling down the aisles.

Everything is so crazy that Rupert forgets to come out as the prince, which is probably okay, since a frog in that kind of shape isn't likely to turn into anything anyway.

"Cut! Cut! Stop!!!" Mrs. Aloi runs out and takes the frog leg from me. "Where's the rest?"

I point to the audience where a first grader has picked it up and is watching more beads spill out of the bottom. "I'll take it home and have my mother sew it back together," I say. "I'll have it waiting in the wishing well for tonight."

Mrs. Aloi smiles. "Your mother sews? I didn't know that."

"My mother is good at a lot of things." Technically, that isn't a lie. I just don't mention that sewing is not one of them.

Besides, it doesn't matter. We already have a new frog.

She's waiting backstage, and she's going to be the star of the show.

chapter 12

Mom's late picking me up because Sparky climbed up into one of the hanging plants on the porch and was swinging there like Tarzan and wouldn't come down.

Things are so busy with homework and dinner that I never even mention the problem with the stuffed frog. It's a good thing because Mom couldn't have fixed it anyway. She's even having trouble pinning the sash on my princess dress.

It takes so long that I'm almost late for "the call." That's the fancy theater name for the time you have to get there if you're in the play.

Mrs. Aloi runs right up to me. "Do you have the frog?"

The frog. "Umm . . ."

"All set!" Rupert steps up and adjusts his crown. "I just put the frog in the wishing well. We're ready."

"Hey, princess!" James steps up and tips my chin into the air a little. I give him my best snooty royal look. "Perfect!"

“Nice job,” I whisper to Rupert. “What did you do, put the whole aquarium in?”

He nods. “There’s just enough room in there for me to crouch down next to it. I’ll hand the frog up to you when it’s time.”

I can’t help grinning, and it’s a Marty grin — not a princess grin. I keep imagining what everyone’s going to do when a real live frog shows up from the wishing well.

“Okay, let’s get quiet, everyone!” James arranges us in a line to head backstage. “This is your big night. Remember, whatever happens, the show goes on. If someone trips or forgets a line, you just keep going. Or improvise — remember? Make something up if you have to. But keep going. You've worked so hard to bring this story to life. Let the magic begin!"

We take our places backstage and I look around in the almost-dark. The scenery crew did a great job painting the big flat panels of wood into a castle. It's set up on one side of the stage, separated from the wishing well by some big cut-out trees.

Tonight, everything really does look magical. Especially the wishing well. I make a quick wish myself — *please let this work* — and then the curtain slides open.

The lights are so bright I feel like I'm looking into the sun. I almost forget to start waltzing for our opening act, but Annie the bluebird nudges me with one of her wings.

I twirl and one-two-three-step with everyone else.

Our first number goes by fast. The forest animals flutter offstage and there I am.

Alone under the lights.

Alone with about a trillion people staring at me.

Alone and way too hot and I can't remember what I'm supposed to say up here.

I toss my golden ball and think,
but the harder I think,
the more thumpy
my heart

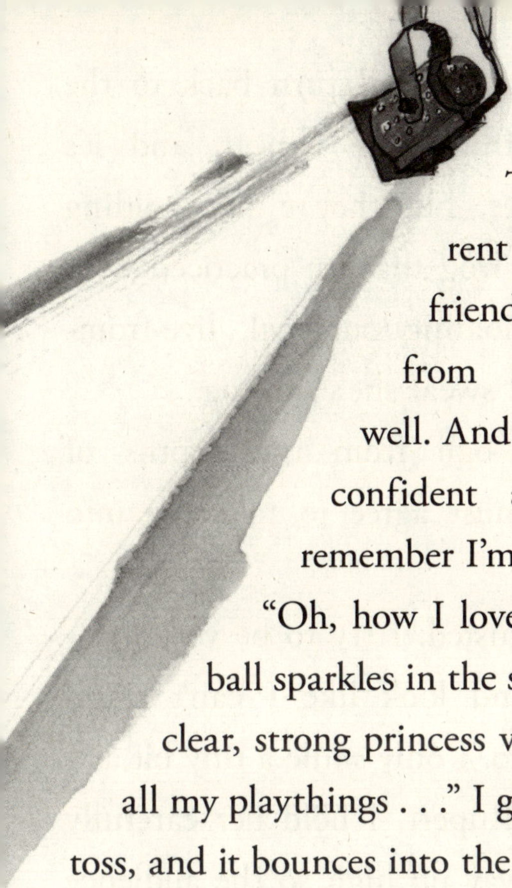

gets and I can't remember anything.

Then I hear a different kind of thump. One friendly frog-jump thump from inside the wishing well. And I remember that I'm confident and brave. And I remember I'm not alone after all.

"Oh, how I love the way my golden ball sparkles in the sunlight," I say in my clear, strong princess voice. "My favorite of all my playthings . . ." I give the ball one more toss, and it bounces into the well.

"Oh no!" I let my mouth drop open, and I feel real tears filling up my eyes. "I've lost my beautiful golden ball in the deep, dark well. Whatever will I do?" I turn away from the well and cry some more.

"Fear not, fair princess." I turn back to the well. It's Rupert's frog voice I hear, and it's Rupert's hands I see, but they're not holding the stuffed beanbag frog that we practiced with all week. They're holding our real, live-from-the-pond frog. And I swear she's smiling.

"I'll fetch your ball from the depths of the well, but you must agree to take me into your home."

I try to look disgusted. I try to be very princessy and snooty and look like I can't stand the frog. Honest, I do. I only smile a tiny bit as I take the frog from Rupert. I hold her carefully under her forelegs, way up high so the audience can see.

I can hear them whispering.

"Is that a *real* frog?"

"It has to be plastic, doesn't it?"

"They'd never allow a real frog."

“Oh my gosh, I think it just blinked.”

“Oh dear, Marty.” I think that last one might have been my mom’s voice, but I can’t be sure because I’ve stepped into my room at the castle.

The king and queen, my parents, are supposed to enter now and talk with me about the promise I made to the frog.

The king enters. Rasheena looks royal and powerful in her crown and big purple cape. She looks at the frog, and her eyebrows shoot up, but then she just smiles and goes right on with her lines. “Greetings, daughter,” she says, and holds out her hand to help the queen step into the room.

The queen enters. “Greetings, my fair daughter. How was your walk in the —”

Veronica Grace spots the frog in my hands and all of a sudden forgets about being the queen. She forgets about her fluffy dress and her glittery shoes and her fancy tiara. She forgets to walk with her nose in the air and her chin held high. She forgets to be graceful and royal. But she remembers how to scream.

"EEEEWWWWW!" She runs offstage and right out the back door to the third-grade hallway, tripping over her high heels and flailing her arms like the twirly things on a windmill. She does not look even a tiny bit royal or graceful.

I try not to laugh, because we're still onstage, but it's hard. And then I look down at the frog. I think she's laughing, too.

I look at Rasheena. She looks at me. Rasheena must have been listening during rehearsal because she improvises perfectly, just like James taught us. "Perhaps the queen is not feeling well," she says.

I smile. "Perhaps not." Then I remember I'm supposed to hate the frog right now, too. "But oh, Father, I have a terrible problem. This creature has come home with me. I promised to take it into the castle after it fetched my golden ball from the well. But alas, I cannot stand to look at it!" I push the frog out toward Rasheena.

She takes it right out of my hands. "Then you must keep your word," she says, and sets the frog down on the chair by the dinner table.

I hold my breath. I didn't think about what would happen when we had to put her down.

Would she jump right off the stage? Would she get stepped on?

Rasheena and I both look down at the frog. She looks up at us. Then she hops up onto the dinner plate next to a plastic chicken drumstick.

The audience laughs.

Rasheena smiles and says her next line. "You must keep your word, princess. Let the frog share your food and your place of rest. Good things come to those who keep their promises. Now come, Queen Margaret. Let us go."

Rasheena turns and leaves. By herself. I guess she practiced that line so many times, she forgot that Queen Margaret ran screaming into the hall a long time ago.

Our frog is a perfect Frog Prince frog. She sits at the dinner plate when she's supposed to sit at the dinner plate.

She looks up at me with huge froggy eyes when I scream my bratty princess scream. "I can't believe there is a frog in my bedroom!"

And when I have to put her onto the pillow on my bed, she sits very quietly and doesn't pee on it or anything. I take a deep breath. This is the part where the princess is the maddest of all.

"Stupid creature! I do not care what my father says. You are a disgusting, worthless frog!" I lift the frog from the pillow and hold it up high. I hear worried whispers from backstage. They all know what happens next.

This is the part where I'm supposed to swing

the frog over my head and fling it against the wall. The part where the stuffed frog lost its stuffing. And everybody whispering backstage gets quiet.

They have no idea that Rupert and I figured out a whole new plan while we were looking for the net in his garage. Is it still improvising if you change things at the last minute but you talked about it ahead of time?

chapter 13

"Wait!" I say, holding the frog higher and turning to face the audience. "Perhaps I have not looked at you closely enough. For now I see how the yellow flecks in your eyes glitter like the sun. They glitter like the precious golden ball you saved for me with your kind, froggy heart."

"In fact . . ." I kneel down, still holding the frog. I pull her in close to my face — so close I can see her nostril holes and the brown flecks in her eyes. I need to just do it before I can think about it anymore. "In fact, my beautiful frog . . . I love you!"

I pucker up and plant a noisy smooch right on the frog's mouth. Sort of. Frogs don't have very big mouths, so I sort of end up kissing her whole face, which isn't slimy at all — just nice and smooth and cool. I don't even mind.

But apparently, the frog does. After all this time sitting still, she wiggles and wriggles and kicks like crazy until I can't hold her anymore. She takes a giant leap that has to be at least twenty times her body length — probably more — and bounds off the stage into the audience. Santjie the South African record-setting frog would be proud.

Only one lady screams — probably Veronica Grace's mom. She jumps from her seat and tears out the back door. Everyone else just sits and watches while the frog takes one perfect leap after another, all the way up the aisle to the very back row of seats and then follows the screaming lady right out the door to the playground.

I'm still kneeling onstage staring when I hear a voice.

"It is me, O kind princess."

"Huh?" I turn, and there's Rupert in his prince outfit. "What are you doing here?"

"Don't you recognize me, princess?" He kicks my foot and says it again. "Don't you recognize your frog prince?"

"Oh yeah!" I say. I forgot about the rest of the play. I guess it never occurred to me that he would still show up. "Well, hi there!"

Rupert frowns. I guess he doesn't appreciate my improvising, so I go back to the real lines. "O handsome prince, I am so glad that you are free from the spell and are no longer a frog."

"Will you marry me?"

"Of course!"

I take Rupert's arm and we walk offstage.

The audience claps and claps. They won't stop. And I don't want them to.

The cast comes back out onstage for the curtain call. My mom and dad are in the front row, clapping like crazy. I look offstage where James and Mrs. Aloi are waiting. They're clapping, too. Mrs. Aloi looks a little ruffled, but James gives me the thumbs-up sign.

"Good improvising!" he yells over the applause.

"Way to go!" Annie ducks in next to me and grabs my hand. "That was awesome!"

"Thanks." I smile at her and squeeze her hand. "You helped, you know."

One by one, the actors and actresses come back to take a bow. Veronica Grace steps out in her fluffy dress and curtsies, and even she gets extra applause. Maybe the audience thought the queen was supposed to run off looking like a

windmill. They clap and cheer, and that makes Veronica Grace so happy she curtsies three more times.

Then she falls in line next to me and it's time for our final bow.

I reach out to her so we can join hands for the bow like we're supposed to, but she scrunches up her face and yanks her hand away.

"Eewww! Frog hands!" She scoots over so she's next to Rupert instead and takes his hand for the final bow. I think about hollering over to her that Rupert has frog hands, too, but I decide not to.

I make one last curtsy as the curtain closes, and the applause is louder than ever.

I sure hope our frog can hear it from the pond.

chapter 14

The very best part of the play isn't that last scene with the frog and Rasheena and Rupert. It isn't the curtain call where we get a standing ovation. It isn't even the cast party, where Mom and Dad aren't paying attention and so I get to have five brownies.

The very best part is Saturday morning after the show. Because just as I'm finishing my French toast with powdery sugar on top, the phone rings.

"Hi, wanna come over and go for a hike in the woods and look for crayfish in the creek and pretend we're Jane Goodall saving the chimpanzees and winning awards for it and stuff?"

Annie's back.

"Hey, Mom!" I find her filling up Sparky's water dish in the kitchen. "Can I go play with Annie?"

"I think so," she says, "but first, Dad and I want to talk with you about last night."

Dad pours coffee for himself and Mom, sits down at the table, and points to the chair across from him. Too bad. Sitting-down talks take longer.

"First of all," Mom says. "We want you to know how proud we were to see you up there onstage last night."

Dad grins. "For somebody who didn't want to be a princess, you were a pretty terrific one."

"Thanks. Can I go to Annie's now?"

I start to stand up, but Mom points me back to my chair. "Not yet. We need to talk about one more thing." She looks at Dad.

"Marty," he says, "even though you did a great job in the play . . . what you did, switching the frog, wasn't very responsible."

"But the old frog was dumb."

"That's not the point," Mom says.

"It had beanbag bits leaking out of its bottom," I say.

"That's still not the point."

"And you don't know how to sew, so you couldn't fix it or anything."

"Marty . . ." Mom puts down her coffee. "You're very lucky things went as well as they did. I know you wanted a real frog, but think about it. That frog could have been hurt. He could have fallen or been stepped on or —"

"She," I say.

"What?"

"The frog. It's not a *he.* It's a *she.* I checked the eardrums."

"Marty, the point is, that poor frog could have been hurt just because you wanted the play to be more interesting," Mom says. "Think about the choices you make, okay?"

"Okay." I really would have felt terrible if anything had happened to our frog.

Mom stands and picks up Sparky's water dish.

"Can I go to Annie's now?"

She smiles. "That would be an excellent choice."

Annie's mom makes pancakes, so I eat breakfast again because it's rude not to eat food that someone makes you, and plus, I love pancakes, so I'm pretty sure that's a good choice, too.

"Want more syrup?" Annie asks. She knows I always do.

"Thanks." I take it and pour a big puddle onto my plate. "I'm glad you're back, Annie."

"Back from where?"

"You know, from dancing lessons and floofy ballerina dresses and dumb stuff like that."

She puts down her fork. "I'm not back from anyplace. I still like all that stuff."

"But I thought you wanted to catch crayfish."

"I do. But I still like dancing and stuff, too. Who says I have to choose?"

"Well . . ." I think about that while I finish my pancake and use my finger to get the last of the syrup. "I guess nobody."

"Good," she says. "You ready?"

We're just about to head outside when the doorbell rings. It's Veronica Grace.

"Hi." She looks down at her shoes. I look, too. It's hard not to look at them, since they are red, sparkly, high-heeled shoes like Dorothy stole from the mean witch in *The Wizard of Oz*.

"Nice ruby slippers," Annie says.

"I . . . um . . . came over to see if you wanted to play dress-up." She looks at Annie.

"No, thanks. Right now, Marty and I are looking for crayfish and pretending we're Jane Goodall saving the chimpanzees."

"Chimpanzees?" Veronica Grace wrinkles her nose.

"It's okay," Annie says. "They're friendly."

"Oh." Veronica Grace looks at her shoes again.

"You want to come with us?" Annie asks her.

No way, I think, but I don't say it out loud because Mom would call that a rude choice and not a good one, probably.

Veronica Grace doesn't look happy about the idea either. She makes a face like she's been invited to jump into a pit full of poisonous snakes. But then she takes a deep breath and says, "Maybe. Can we do dress-up stuff, too?"

I look down at her fancy-tippy shoes. She'll never be able to keep up with the chimpanzees. "There's no way you can wear those out to the creek," I say. "It's all rocky and muddy out there. You need sneakers or hiking boots like these." I balance on one foot and hold up the other one so she can see the new chimpanzee-saving boots Mom got me when school started.

"Could she borrow your old mud shoes, Marty? You left them here over the summer," Annie says. She digs my used-to-be-white sneakers out of the shoe closet and holds them up. They're brownish-grayish-greenish now. And kind of smelly, even from the other side of the room.

Veronica Grace wrinkles her nose.

"Oh, come on," I say. "Improvise."

"Fine," she says, and pulls off her sparkly ruby shoes. She picks up the first sneaker and tries to put it on without really touching it, which takes forever.

"You know, you can't be Princess Bossy-Pants if you're going to come with us," I say.

Oops.

"Sorry," I add quietly.

Veronica Grace doesn't say anything, but she gives up on not touching the mud shoes, laces them up, and looks down at her brownish-grayish-greenish feet.

"There," she says. "No more tippy shoes." Then she reaches into her bag and pulls out some jeweled tiaras. "But these should be okay, right?"

"Sure!" Annie takes one and puts it on her head. "We'll be the queens of the rain forest."

Veronica Grace holds another one out to me.

"Oh, all right." I put it on. I've never seen Jane Goodall wearing one of these, but even scientists have to improvise sometimes.

Just as we're cutting through the vegetable garden that Annie's mom and my mom share, our front door opens and Dad bends down in his bathrobe to pick up the newspaper.

A crazy fast flash of black-brown-gray fur whips past him and sends the paper flying out of his hand. Dad loses his balance and falls into the juniper bush by the steps. The black-brown-gray flash zooms over to the pine tree in the front yard and climbs up.

"Sparky!" Mom calls from the door. Then she sees Dad in the bush. "Oh. Sorry. Do you think you can help me get her down?"

"Rachel," Dad says, pulling little green needles out of his pajama bottoms. "Do you really think that raccoon still needs to be saved? Take a look."

Mom looks up. Sparky's more than halfway up the tree, out on a wide branch. She throws down a pinecone. It bounces off Mom's forehead.

"I guess maybe Sparky's all better," she says, and heads back inside with Dad.

Annie, Veronica Grace, and I wave to Sparky and head for the woods.

"After we save the chimpanzees," Annie says, "we'll have a ceremony, and we'll all win the Nobel Peace Prize."

"Oooh, a ceremony!" Veronica Grace gives a little hop. "That means fancy gowns and dancing!"

Annie gives me a hopeful smile.

"Oh, all right," I say, starting down the path to the woods. I guess I can improvise a little, too.

Turn the page for a sneak peek at Marty's next adventure:

marty mcguire digs worms!

As soon as I see the blackboard in my classroom Monday morning, I can tell it is going to be an extra-super week. There are three terrific things on Mrs. Aloi's "Third Grade Stars Today" list.

1. Today is Monday!

Even though my dad likes Fridays best, I think Mondays are way better. We have library on Mondays, and if you tell Ms. Stephanie about the last book you read, she gives you a Starburst from her secret stash under the librarian desk. Plus Mondays are goulash days in the cafeteria, which would be awful except that they serve ice cream cups for dessert because who would buy goulash if you weren't getting ice cream with it? So Mondays are very tasty days.

2. Classroom helper this week is Marty McGuire!

I love being classroom helper because when you are classroom helper, you don't have to sit still so much. You get to hand out papers and pick up papers and be line leader and take the lunch count down to the cafeteria all by yourself or with a friend. I'm going to ask Annie to go with me. Plus you get to feed Horace, our class lizard. You have to remember to put the lid back on the jar of crickets when you're done or they get out and hop down the hall and scare Miss Gail, the art teacher.

3. We will have a special assembly before lunch!

When we have an assembly, we get to go to the auditorium with everyone in the whole school and sit in the springy chairs where the bottom folds up and shuts you right up inside if you're not careful. That hasn't happened to me since kindergarten. At assemblies, an Interesting Person comes and talks instead of teachers. One time, the Interesting Person brought pythons and told us all about where pythons live and what they eat. One time, the Interesting Person brought costumes from a long time ago and let us try them on. And one time, three Interesting People came and rode unicycles right across the stage and didn't crash into one another even once. I wonder who it will be today.

The fourth thing on the "Third Grade Stars Today" list is not so terrific.

4. First job today: math work sheet!

How exactly does a math work sheet deserve an exclamation point? I can see why Mrs. Aloi would put an exclamation point after the assembly or me being classroom helper or Starburst-and-ice-cream Monday. But a math work sheet?

Math work sheets barely deserve a period and for sure not an exclamation point.

"Mrs. Aloi?" Veronica Grace says. "What's the assembly going to be about? There aren't going to be snakes again, are there?" Veronica Grace does not like snakes or anything else that slithers or crawls.

"No, Veronica Grace. Not today."

"Awwww," says Rupert Wingfield. I look over at him and grin. I liked the snake lady, too.

"I hope we get somebody good," says Jimmy Lawson. "I hope it's that guy from the TV show where they drop him off in the wilderness and he has to survive. He could come in and eat bugs like he did on TV."

"Ewww!" says Veronica Grace.

"Hey!" Alex Farley jumps out of his seat and knocks his tool belt against his desk. "Maybe it'll be Mick Buzzsaw, that guy from *Handyman America*! He can build a swing-set right up on stage like he did on his show."

"Maybe it'll be somebody from the Nature Channel," says Annie.

"Maybe it'll be Lola Smitterly from *Dance-o-Rama*!" says Kimmy Butler.

"Ohh!" Veronica Grace says. "And maybe she'll bring cameras and put us on TV!"

Mrs. Aloi shakes her maracas. "It's time for us to go to the auditorium now. The guest for our assembly is a very special visitor who's here to talk with us about keeping the earth healthy. Line up, and remember to set a good example for the kindergartners."

I lead the class to the auditorium and go all the way down to the end of the front row like I'm supposed to. I keep both feet on the floor, and I don't twist around in my seat. I watch the first and second graders and kindergartners find their seats. I wonder if our assembly person will be worth that exclamation point.